AMERICA GOES TO WAR

THE AMERICAN REVOLUTION

TIMELINES, FACTS, AND BATTLES

By Craig Boutland

Published in 2023 by The Rosen Publishing Group, Inc.
2544 Clinton Street, Buffalo, NY 14224

Editor: Lindsey Lowe
Children's Publisher: Anne O'Daly
Design Manager: Keith Davis
Picture Manager: Sophie Mortimer

Picture Credits:
Front Cover: Public Domain
Key: t = top, b = bottom, c = center
Alamy: Artokoloro 24, ClassicStock 18, Granger Collection 27, 51t, Historical Picture Archive 26t, Photo12 17c, Science History Images 61t, Stocktrek Images Inc 51b, Universal Images Group 21, Wetdryvac 25; Bridgeman Images: 19, 42; Getty Images: Burstein Collection 6; Library of Congress: 16-17b, 31, 34, 34-35, 40-41, 56, 60; Look and Learn: 8b; Metropolitan Museum of Art: 33, 39, 52-53; National Portrait Gallery: 23b, 35b; Public Domain: 7, 11t, 22b, 23t, 44b, 49, 50, 52t, Alonzo Chapell 14t, British Library 47c, debaird 47b, Granger Collection 11c, Joconde/Palace of Versailles 53t, library.brown.edu 45, Mwanner 29t, National Guard Bureau 10-11, New York Public Library 10, 28, 29c, 32t, 32b, 40-41c, Royal Academy 46-47, si.unich.edu 35t, SimonandSchuster 44t, Smithsonian 17t, Smithsonianmag 12, 54, the Gallery Collection 9, Yale Center for British Art, Paul Mellon Collection 13, Yale University Art Gallery 40; Robert Hunt Library: 48; Thinkstock; 5, 20, 37, 41t, 55; Topfoto: Alinari Archives 30, Granger Collection 16-17t, 38, 58, 61b; U.S. Government: aoc.gov 57, Capitol 23c, 36, National Park Service 15,46, 52b, 22t, White House 17b; U.S. National Archives: 35c, 41b, 47t, 59.

Cataloging-in-Publication Data

Names: Boutland, Craig.
Title: The American Revolution: timeline, facts, and battles / Craig Boutland.
Description: New York : Rosen Publishing, 2023. | Series: America goes to war| Includes bibliographic references, index and glossary.
Identifiers: ISBN 9781499473827 (pbk) | ISBN 9781499473834 (library bound) | ISBN 9781499473841 (ebook)
Subjects: LCSH: United States—History—Revolution, 1775-1783— Juvenile literature
Classification: LCC E208 B68 2023 | DDC 973.3—dc23

Manufactured in the United States of America

CPSIA Compliance Information: Batch #CWRYA23. For further information contact Rosen Publishing at 1-800-237-9932.

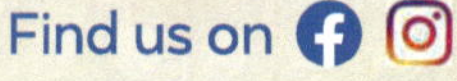

CONTENTS

Introduction

The Revolution began as a rebellion against laws and taxation imposed by the British. It ended as a determined effort to escape British rule altogether.

When the war began in 1775, many Americans did not want independence—they only wanted the British to take their grievances seriously. They believed they should be represented in the British Parliament in London. In the face of British resistance, however, the majority of settlers in Britain's 13 colonies became convinced that independence would be necessary.

The Course of the War

When New England militia fired on British troops at Lexington on April 19, 1775, America did not possess an army or even a single leader. Within a few years, however, it had created a force that could defeat the British army, at the time the strongest in the world. It was led by a volunteer who would become the first president of the new nation: George Washington.

To begin with, the British believed they would soon put down the rebellion. But American resistance by disorganized militia turned into American aggression by a disciplined army, which inflicted a significant defeat on the British at the Battle of Saratoga in October 1777. Another British army remained, farther south, but after more years of fighting, the Americans managed to trap and defeat it at Yorktown. Meanwhile, the colonial leaders had declared independence and announced the creation of a new nation: the United States of America.

About This Book

This book contains two types of timelines. Along the bottom of the pages is a timeline that covers the whole period. It lists key events and developments, color coded to indicate their part in the war. Each chapter also has its own timeline, which runs vertically down the sides of the pages. This timeline gives more specific information about the particular subject of the chapter. IN FOCUS spreads detail personalities, events, and key topics.

George Washington (in black cloak) prepares to receive the British surrender at the Battle of Yorktown in 1781.

Causes of the War

The American colonies had clashed with their British rulers for a number of years before the situation deteriorated dramatically and war became inevitable.

➔ This picture shows British troops opening fire on a crowd during the so-called Boston Massacre in 1770.

TIMELINE **1770–1772**

KEY: Politics | Northern Campaign | Southern Campaign

1770

January 28, 1770 London
Lord Frederick North becomes prime minister in Britain.

March 5, 1770 Boston
British troops open fire on a crowd, killing five people in the "Boston Massacre."

April 12, 1770 London
British Parliament repeals duties on paper, glass, and other commodities in the American colonies, but retains tax on tea.

1771

The roots of the Revolutionary War lie in British history. In 1689, the English Parliament was given, for the first time, the right to review all new laws and taxes requested by the king. In England's American colonies, settlers believed the y should have the same rights as people in England. Their colonial assemblies, however, had no right to review laws and taxes.

In the early 1700s, England, Wales, and Scotland united to form Great Britain. When Britain went to war with France, its colonies in North America fought, too. The wars were expensive, and the British needed to raise as much money as possible to pay for them.

When the wars ended in 1763, the British imposed taxes on the American colonists. Many colonists thought this was unfair and avoided paying them as much as they could. There were riots against the British. On March 5, 1770, British troops opened fire on a crowd of protestors in Boston, killing five civilians.

KEY DATES

March 18, 1765 The British Parliament passes the Stamp Act, taxing colonists directly for the first time.

March 5, 1770 In the Boston Massacre, British troops fire a musket volley into a crowd of Bostonians, killing five people.

December 16, 1773 The Boston Tea Party involves protesters boarding a British tea ship ad throwing tea into the harbor.

March 31, 1774 Coercive Acts (Intolerable Acts) see Britain close Boston Harbor and take other repressive actions.

September 5, 1774 The Continental Congress, drawn from 12 of the colonies, meets for the first time in Philadelphia.

← The unpopular Stamp Act of March 1765 placed a direct tax on colonists for the first time.

1772

November 1772 Massachusetts Samuel Adams forms the Committees of Correspondence in Massachusetts to coordinate action against the British.

November 1772 Massachusetts The Boston Assembly demands rights for the colonies and threatens to leave the empire if these are refused.

George III (1738–1820)

George III became king of England in 1760. He wanted the monarchy to have more authority over government policy. This immediately brought him into conflict with Parliament. In 1770, George made Lord Frederick North prime minister. North shared the king's belief that Parliament should make laws for the American colonies, rather than let the colonies do it.

George III refused to acknowledge the complaints of the American colonists.

This cartoon urges the colonies to unite to defeat the British.

The Boston Tea Party

Tea had been popular in Europe since the 17th century and was also popular in the colonies. When the British tried to import untaxed tea from India to sell cheaply, colonists worried that it would become more difficult for colonial merchants to sell their own tea. Bostonians boarded a ship and threw 342 casks of tea into the harbor on December 16, 1773.

Intolerable Acts

This so-called Boston Tea Party led to what colonists called the Intolerable Acts. In an effort to stop dissent from spreading through New England, the British closed the port of Boston and put Massachusetts under royal government. British soldiers began seizing stores of supplies held for use by the colonial militia. These groups of citizen soldiers provided the colonies' main form of defense. Without an armed

TIMELINE 1773–1774

KEY: Politics | Northern Campaign | Southern Campaign

1773

March 12, 1773 Virginia
Virginia establishes a Committee of Correspondence.

December 16, 1773 Massachusetts
At the Boston Tea Party, Patriots throw a cargo of tea overboard from a British ship.

1774

militia, the colonies would not be in a position to defend themselves against the British. By the spring of 1775, the thirteen colonies were in a state of great tension. Years of clashes between colonists and British authorities had culminated in violence at Boston. However, many Americans called for a peaceful resolution to the crisis.

Countdown to War

The thought of war between Britain and its colonies was shocking to people on both sides of the Atlantic Ocean. Yet the determination of the British government to impose its will on the troublesome colonies, and the equally strong resolve in the colonies to resist this at all costs, made conflict inescapable. All that was needed was a spark to ignite it, and this soon came.

Continental Congress

The Continental Congress met in the Philadelphia State House in 1774. Representatives came from twelve colonies. Congress agreed to stop buying British goods and demanded that Britain undo its new laws. Congress agreed to meet again in May 1775 to decide what action to take. By then, however, fighting had begun in Massachusetts. The Congress continued to meet until 1789 and acted as the colonies' governing body during the Revolution.

Protestors throw tea overboard at the Boston Tea Party.

March–May 1774 Massachusetts
Britain's Coercive Acts (Intolerable Acts) against Massachusetts include the indefinite closure of the port of Boston.

September 5, 1774 Philadelphia
Delegates from all the colonies except Georgia meet at the First Continental Congress.

September 17, 1774 Massachusetts
In the Suffolk Resolves, Committees of Correspondence decide to ignore the Coercive Acts, marking an increase in tension.

October

December 1, 1774 North America
Approved by the First Continental Congress, a boycott on any imports from Britain to the American colonies comes into effect.

Colonial Militias and Minutemen

The militias of the thirteen colonies had a long history and were to prove resolute in the face of the British Army.

Militias had been formed in Britain's North American colonies in the 17th century. In the colony of Massachusetts, for example, all able-bodied men between 16 and 60 were required to serve in the militia. This militia was a force intended to defend against Native American raids. The militiamen trained a number of times per year, and the younger and best of them were soon formed into bands that could serve at short notice—the aptly named "Minutemen." About a third of the militia were designated Minutemen; they provided their own weapons, which could be anything from a hunting rifle to a type of scatter-shot blunderbuss.

1

Lexington and Concord

As tensions with the British government grew during the early 1770s, Minutemen companies trained more frequently and became a focus of Patriot sentiment. The Massachusetts Provincial Congress reorganized the militia in 1774. Minutemen elected their own officers and comprised about a quarter of the militia as a whole. They took on the British troops that marched on Lexington and Concord, forcing them to retreat, and so began the open warfare of the American Revolution. The British regulars were trained to fight in long disciplined lines, and during the retreat found it difficult to cope with the tactics of the Minutemen, who fired from behind cover and moved to new locations from where they could pick off the British "redcoats."

2

KEY DATES

1637 Colonial militias are raised to fight Native Americans during the Pequot War.

1676 Benjamin Church forms the first Ranger company to defend Plymouth Colony.

1689-1697 Provincial troops raised in Massachusetts form the bulk of the army fighting the French.

1751 Major Robert Rogers organizes nine Ranger companies. They will fight extensively in the French and Indian War of 1754-1763.

1754 George Washington leads the Virginia militia against French and Native American forces.

1774 Massachusetts decides to reorganize its militia, and formalizes the establishment of Minutemen in companies of at least 50 men, ready for action at any time. They will elect their own officers.

1 Colonel Benjamin Church. He formed the first Ranger company as part of the defense of Plymouth Colony.

2 A modern representation of the first militias being drilled in the use of firearms and infantry tactics.

3 A 17th-century print of colonial militia firing volleys against Native Americans in defence of their settlement.

4 The great fear of early colonists was to be surprised and slaughtered by a sudden Native American attack.

Lexington and Concord

The colonists responded to the attempt to enforce the unpopular Coercive (Intolerable) Acts by attacking British troops and forcing them to retreat.

A painting depicting Paul Revere's "midnight ride" on April 18, 1775, to warn the colonists.

TIMELINE **1775 JANUARY–JUNE**

KEY:  **Politics** **Northern Campaign** **Southern Campaign**

January

March 25 Virginia
Patrick Henry makes his "liberty or death" speech to the Second Virginia Convention.

March 30 London
The New England Restraining Act forces New England colonies to trade only with England.

April 14 Massachusetts
Governor Thomas Gage is secretly ordered by the British to enforce the Coercive Acts and use force to put down "open revolution."

April 18 Massachusetts
Thomas Gage sends 700 British soldiers to Concord to destroy militia weapons stores. Paul Revere makes his midnight ride to warn colonists in Lexington.

The first shots in the Revolutionary War were fired on April 19, 1775, in a series of skirmishes known as the Battles of Lexington and Concord. Fighting broke out when the British military governor of Massachusetts, General Thomas Gage, received orders to seize the stores of arms and ammunition that Patriots, as the American colonists became known, had stockpiled at Concord, west of Boston.

A Midnight Dash

On the night of April 18, a force of some 700 British redcoats crossed Boston Harbor, landed at Phipps Farm, south of the road to Cambridge, and marched toward Concord. They planned to stop off at Lexington on the way to arrest two prominent Patriot leaders, Samuel Adams and John Hancock.

Thomas Gage was the unpopular military governor of Massachusetts.

KEY DATES

April 14, 1775 Governor Gage is secretly ordered to enforce the Coercive (Intolerable) Acts and suppress any rebellions, using force if necessary.

April 18, 1775 Gage orders 700 British soldiers to Concord to destroy weapons stores of the colonial militia.

April 18, 1775 Paul Revere sets off on horseback to warn the colonists.

April 19, 1775 A shot starts the Revolutionary War. British troops are forced back from Lexington to Boston. Farmers and militia fire on them throughout their retreat.

April 19, 1775 Patriot siege of Boston begins.

April 21, 1775 New Hampshire militia march to Cambridge, Massachusetts, after hearing about Lexington and Concord.

April 19 Massachusetts
The first shots are fired at Lexington and Concord. British troops retreat to Boston, where they are besieged. News of the insurrection spreads rapidly.

May 10 New York
Forces led by Ethan Allen and Benedict Arnold capture Fort Ticonderoga, New York, which has military supplies; the Second Continental Congress meets in Philadelphia.

May 17 Canada
Troops led by Benedict Arnold capture St. John's in Canada.

June

June 14 Philadelphia
Congress establishes the Continental Army; the next day, George Washington is appointed commander in chief.

June 17 Massachusetts
In the Battle of Bunker Hill at Boston, the British capture the hill but lose half of their men.

Paul Revere (1735–1818)

Paul Revere was a Boston silversmith and dedicated Patriot. He gathered intelligence about British soldiers, which he passed on to Patriot leaders. At around 10:00 p.m. on April 18, 1775, he rode to Lexington to warn Samuel Adams and John Hancock of the impending arrival of British troops. His ride was made famous in a poem by Henry Wadsworth Longfellow.

→ Patriots drive redcoats from the North Bridge in Concord.

Despite their precautions, the British soldiers were spotted. Two messengers set out to warn Adams, Hancock, and the militia guarding the arms store in Concord of the British approach. A young shoemaker, William Dawes, rode off across Boston Neck, while silversmith Paul Revere took a faster route across the water to Charlestown. By the time the British reached Lexington, around dawn, Adams and Hancock had escaped. The redcoats were met on Lexington Green by 77 Minutemen under the command of Captain John Parker. The British ordered the Americans to disperse.

→ Paul Revere's midnight ride is celebrated by this statue in Boston.

TIMELINE **1775 JULY–DECEMBER**

KEY: Politics | Northern Campaign | Southern Campaign

July

July 3 Massachusetts
George Washington takes command of the Continental army and 17,000 troops around Boston.

August 22 London
King George III issues a proclamation declaring the American colonies to be in a state of open rebellion against the Crown.

September 25 Canada
Ethan Allen aborts his attack on Montreal and is captured by the British.

The Patriots began to give way—but then shooting broke out. No one knows who fired the "shot heard round the world," as the contemporary Patriot author Tom Paine called it—both sides claimed that the other fired first. The redcoats then fired a volley and made a bayonet charge. The outnumbered Americans ran for cover, leaving eight dead and ten wounded. One British soldier was hurt. The British commander ordered his men to stop firing and march on to Concord.

A Second Shot

The British arrived in Concord at 8:00 a.m. and began looking for the arms, most of which had already been spirited away. Again a single shot rang out, this time by the North Bridge. Once again, the British soldiers returned fire without waiting for orders. This time the local militia did not run; instead, they fired back. At noon, the British commander decided to retreat to Boston.

On the long march back, the weary British were fired on by Patriots from behind walls, hedges, and boulders. During the day's fighting, the British lost 273 men and the Americans 95. The action caused a surge of military enthusiasm that led to the siege of Boston; the Revolutionary War had begun.

Sam Adams (1722-1803)

Sam Adams was born in Boston, a relative of the later President of the United States, John Adams. A member of the Massachusetts House of Representatives, Sam was a leading opponent of British taxes, and organized resistance through corresponding societies and getting crowds onto the streets. He helped draft the Articles of Confederation and was an important proponent of the Declaration of Independence. He later became the Governor of Massachusetts.

←Sam Adams led Massachusetts resistance to British policies in the build up to the Revolution.

November

December

November 2 Canada Under General Montgomery, Americans end siege of St. John's and take this important fort.

November 13 Canada After an easy battle, American troops capture and occupy Montreal.

November 28 Philadelphia The Continental Congress establishes an American navy.

December 31 Canada Montgomery is killed during a failed American assault on Quebec.

George Washington

An experienced soldier, Washington took over the army of the thirteen colonies in 1775.

George Washington (1732–1799) was asked to command the army of the Continental Congress in June 1775. He had been a landowner in Virginia who had steadily extended his land and wealth over the previous decade. In 1754 he had commanded British forces that fired the first shots in the French and Indian War. He was a prominent opponent of British acts such as the Intolerable Acts, and was a member of the Second Continental Congress that met inside Independence Hall in 1775 to prepare for war.

Victory and Resignation

Washington's first achievement was to take Boston from British forces in March 1776, but later that year his army was forced out of New York, although he managed to defeat British forces at Trenton in December. Over the next two years, he found it difficult to hold his army together. The British entered Philadelphia and harsh winter conditions led to losses and desertions from the Continental Army. Washington kept it together, however, and French intervention in the war eventually led to the British surrender at Yorktown in 1781. Washington resigned his command in 1783 and returned to civilian life. He became the first president of the United States on April 30, 1789, and again voluntarily resigned after he had served two terms of office.

1

2

KEY DATES

February 22, 1732 George Washington is born in Popes Creek, Westmoreland County, Virginia.

1752 Washington is given a commission in the Virginia militia.

June 15, 1775 Washington is asked to command the newly created army of the Continental Congress, mainly because of his previous military experience and his good character. He refuses to take a salary.

1776–1777 Washington wins victories at Trenton and Princeton, showing that his force can hold its own against the British. This is an important boost to Patriot morale.

October 19, 1781 Washington accepts British surrender at Yorktown.

December 14, 1799 George Washington dies at Mount Vernon, his estate in Virginia.

1 Washington inspects his troops during the bitterly cold winter at Valley Forge, when provisions were in short supply.

2 Washington, on horseback, directs his troops during an encounter in the French and Indian War.

3 Washington resigns his commission as head of the army of the Continental Congress after victory in the Revolutionary War.

4 The young George Washington during the 1750s, when he was a successful plantation owner and tasted his first military action.

5 Washington in 1776, during the period when he was struggling to hold together his army and victory seemed far off.

Battle of Bunker Hill

Although the British won the Battle of Bunker Hill, it was a costly victory. Their casualties were high and American losses were far fewer.

This painting shows the death of Patriot general Joseph Warren at Bunker Hill.

TIMELINE **1776 JANUARY–JUNE**

KEY: Politics | Northern Campaign | Southern Campaign

February 27 North Carolina
A Patriot victory at the Battle of Moore's Creek Bridge boosts morale in the South.

February 29 London
British House of Commons approves the use of German troops in Revolutionary War.

January

March 17 Boston
British evacuate Boston following a heavy artillery bombardment by the Americans.

On June 17, 1775, the bloodiest single engagement of the Revolutionary War took place on the Charlestown peninsula, across the bay from Boston.

Fighting for Position

By the middle of June 1775, 15,000 American men-at-arms had converged on Boston. More than 5,000 British troops, under the command of General Thomas Gage, were under siege in the city. When a rumor reached the Americans that Gage intended to occupy Bunker Hill, Colonel William Prescott was dispatched with 1,200 men to stop him. Prescott's forces dug themselves in on Breed's Hill, next to Bunker Hill, on the night of June 16, 1775.

KEY DATES

April 19, 1775 Siege of Boston begins.

May 10, 1775 Militia seizes Fort Ticonderoga, near Lake Champlain in New York.

June 13, 1775 Patriots learn of General Gage's decision to occupy Dorchester Heights.

June 15, 1775 Congress votes to appoint George Washington general and commander in chief of new Continental Army.

June 17, 1775 Fighting between British and American troops in the Battle of Bunker Hill sees British lose half their force.

March 4, 1776 Washington occupies Dorchester Heights and fortifies it with artillery from Fort Ticonderoga.

March 17, 1776 The British begin an evacuation of Boston.

← British troops land in Boston in 1768 in this painting from the period.

April

June

May 2 France King Louis XVI approves the sending of secret financial aid to support the Patriots.

June 18 Canada General Sullivan evacuates his American troops from Canada to Fort Ticonderoga.

June 21 Philadelphia Thomas Jefferson shows Continental Congress his first draft of the Declaration of Independence.

June 28 South Carolina British attack on Moultrie's Fort on Sullivan's Island ends in total failure with heavy losses.

The next morning, Gage ordered warships in Boston Harbor to shell Prescott's positions. When that failed to dislodge the Americans, he sent Major General William Howe with 2,500 redcoats to secure the peninsula.

A Moral Victory

Covered by artillery fire, the British landed on the peninsula unopposed. When they charged Breed's Hill, however, the enemy was waiting. An American officer ordered, "Don't fire, boys, until you can see the whites of their eyes!" Taking heavy casualties, the redcoats retreated to regroup. By the third British assault, ammunition was running out for the Americans, and the British finally managed to overwhelm the fortifications. The Americans retreated in an orderly fashion under cover from reinforcements brought up by General Israel Putnam of Connecticut.

The Battle of Bunker Hill may have been a victory for the British,

Henry Knox's Winter March

At Fort Ticonderoga in New York, Patriot militia seized artillery needed by the Continental Army. A Boston bookseller, Henry Knox, offered to bring the guns to Boston. Knox and his men took apart the 59 guns and moved them on an arduous 300-mile (480 km) journey along rivers and across the snowy land. George Washington set up the guns in Boston in early March 1776, leaving the British no choice but to evacuate the city.

➔ Knox's march is remembered as one of the great feats of the early Revolution.

TIMELINE 1776 JULY–DECEMBER

KEY: Politics | Northern Campaign | Southern Campaign

July

July 4 Philadelphia
Continental Congress approves Jefferson's Declaration of Independence.

July 9 New York
George Washington orders the Declaration of Independence to be read to the army.

August

August 27 New York
A quick and comprehensive British victory occurs at the Battle of Long Island.

September 9 Philadelphia
By order of Congress, the colonies are to be known as the United States from now on.

The fighting on Breed's Hill was recorded in this drawing of the time.

but it was a victory bought at high cost. There were over a thousand redcoat casualties (including nearly 100 officers killed), while American losses were fewer than half that number: about 450 killed, wounded, or captured. The battle was significant because it was a clear demonstration to the British of the fighting qualities of their inexperienced opponents, whom the British had so far underestimated.

For the Americans, this first major battle against the British may have ended in defeat, but they could claim it as a moral victory. The Battle of Bunker Hill has since been honored as one of the most glorious episodes in the annals of American military history.

The Siege of Boston

Some months after the Battle of Bunker Hill, on March 4, 1776, George Washington occupied Dorchester Heights, overlooking Boston, in a single night. From the heights, Washington could bombard the British inside the city with artillery brought from Fort Ticonderoga. British officers, knowing that Boston could not be held, evacuated the city, ending the siege that had started on April 19, 1775, when the British had retreated to Boston after the Battles of Lexington and Concord.

October

December

October 11–13 New York
Battle of Valcour Island is one of the first fought by the American navy.

October 28 New York
The Battle of White Plains ends with a British victory, with losses on both sides.

November 16 New York
The British capture Fort Washington and now control all of Manhattan Island.

December 8 Delaware
Washington and his men cross the Delaware River into Pennsylvania.

December 26 Trenton
Washington's surprise attack on Hessian forces at Trenton ends in victory and is a morale boost for the Americans.

Declaration of Independence

The Declaration of Independence set out what the thirteen colonies were fighting for in the Revolutionary War.

When the colonists first pushed back against British government taxes they were not claiming that they wanted to be independent. They wanted to have a say in how they were governed, not to create a new state.

During the first year of warfare, however, it became clear that there could be no way back. The writer Thomas Paine published his pamphlet "Common Sense" in January 1776. This made the case for independence and encouraged many who had not dared to suggest it previously. At the same time, King George III made it clear that he had no sympathy for the colonists, and that they could expect to be treated as traitors if they lost the war.

Public opinion then moved rapidly in favor of the colonies declaring themselves free of all British influence. A convention in Virginia declared "the United Colonies free and independent States, absolved from all allegiance to, or dependence upon, the Crown or Parliament of Great Britain."

A Model for the World

Some of the colonies represented at the Continental Congress, such as New York and Pennsylvania, were resistant to the idea of independence. But Pennsylvania changed its mind, and then British forces moved into New York City and the New York Provincial Congress was unable to oppose the declaration. Finally, the Continental Congress approved the declaration on July 4.

With its powerful yet simple language, the American Declaration of Independence from Britain became the model for many other countries that were struggling to assert their independence over the following centuries.

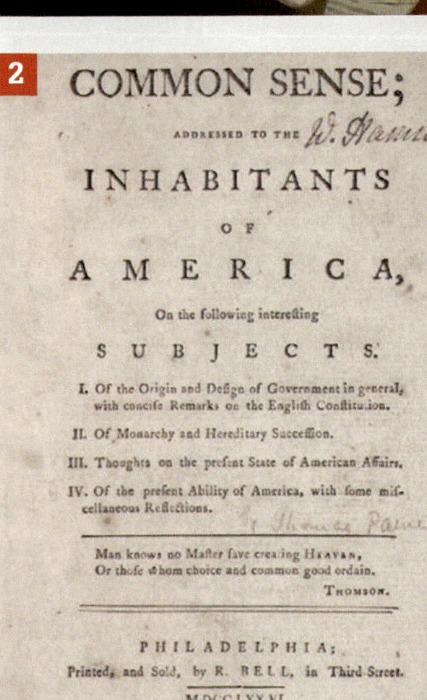

COMMON SENSE;

ADDRESSED TO THE

INHABITANTS

OF

AMERICA,

On the following interesting

SUBJECTS.

I. Of the Origin and Design of Government in general, with concise Remarks on the English Constitution.

II. Of Monarchy and Hereditary Succession.

III. Thoughts on the present State of American Affairs.

IV. Of the present Ability of America, with some miscellaneous Reflections.

Man knows no Master save creating HEAVEN,
Or those whom choice and common good ordain.

THOMSON.

PHILADELPHIA;
Printed, and Sold, by R. BELL, in Third-Street.
MDCCLXXVI.

3

IN CONGRESS, JULY 4, 1776.

The unanimous Declaration of the thirteen united States of America,

KEY DATES

1774 Patriots such as Thomas Jefferson and Samuel Adams argue that the legislatures of the colonies are independent of the parliament in London and owe allegiance to the king only.

September, 1774 The First Continental Congress petitions the king for repeal of the Coercive Acts, known as the Intolerable Acts.

October 26, 1775 Having issued a Proclamation of Rebellion, George III declares he will ask for "offers of foreign assistance" to put down the rebellion. He begins hiring German mercenaries.

April-July 1776 Local associations in the thirteen colonies pass 90 declarations calling for independence.

June 11, 1776 Thomas Jefferson is appointed to a Committee of Five who undertake the writing of the Declaration of Independence.

July 4, 1776 The Declaration of Independence is signed by 56 members of the Second Continental Congress.

1 Thomas Jefferson. He was the principal author of the declaration, and had been recommended for this by John Adams.

2 Thomas Paine's "Common Sense." This pamphlet argued forcefully that the thirteen colonies needed to break free from Britain.

3 The declaration, signed by 56 of the Founding Fathers after Jefferson's original document was edited and shortened.

4 The declaration is presented to the Continental Congress by the Committee of Five who had been asked to create it.

5 Thomas Paine played not only an important part in the American Revolution, but he was also active in the 1790s in the politics of the French Revolution.

Canada

The American Patriots hoped to persuade the Canadian people to join their cause against their colonial rulers. The Patriots were to be disappointed.

The Patriot general Richard Montgomery died at the start of the battle for Quebec.

TIMELINE **1777 JANUARY–JUNE**

KEY: Politics | Northern Campaign | Southern Campaign

January

January 3 New Jersey
Washington's timely arrival stops defeat. The Battle of Princeton ends in an American victory.

January 6 New Jersey
Washington's army encamps for the winter around Morristown.

January 28 England
General John Burgoyne submits a plan to isolate New England from Canada.

March

March 8 New Jersey
General William Maxwell defeats the British at Amboy.

As the Revolution began, Canadians generally rejected the arguments of the American Patriots. The Americans, meanwhile, distrusted the Canadians and their British rulers. The British had taken control of the former French colony of Quebec in 1763, and the Americans had little in common with their French-speaking neighbors. In 1774, the British passed the Quebec Act, which the Americans saw as another Intolerable Act. The act gave freedom of worship to French Catholics. It also allowed the expansion of the province of Quebec westward—into territory that was also targeted for expansion by the thirteen colonies.

Heading North

After the Patriot capture of Fort Ticonderoga on Lake Champlain, New York, on May 10, 1775,

KEY DATES

1760 New France falls.

1763 Proclamation of Quebec assumes Quebec will be like other British-controlled territories.

1774 British Parliament passes the Quebec Act that allows the French majority to carry on with French laws and religion. It also expands its territorial claim into the American West.

May 10, 1775 Americans successfully attack Fort Ticonderoga.

November 13, 1775 Montreal falls to the Americans with no loss of life.

December 31, 1775 Americans fail to take Quebec. Their commander, General Richard Montgomery, is killed, and Arnold takes over.

Summer 1776 American armies withdraw from Canada.

← Britain's Canadian colony lay just north of the American colonies.

April 14 Philadelphia
Congress authorizes the establishment of Springfield Arsenal at Springfield, Massachusetts. It will play a role in Shays' Rebellion.

June 14 Philadephia
Congress adopts stars and stripes as flag with thirteen stars and thirteen stripes for the thirteen colonies.

April

June

April 21–28 Connecticut
British destroy the town of Danbury, burning houses, barns, and storehouses.

Benedict Arnold (1741–1801)

Benedict Arnold joined the Patriot army when the Revolutionary War began. In 1775 he led troops that captured Fort Ticonderoga. His most important contribution was during the defeat of General Burgoyne at the battle of Saratoga. In 1780 he was in command of West Point, and offered to turn it over to the British for £20,000. The plot was discovered and he fled to British lines.

Patriots charge in fierce fighting around Fort Ticonderoga.

the way to Canada was open. An army led by General Richard Montgomery headed north but was delayed by British resistance at the siege of St. John's. When Montgomery finally reached Montreal in November, the city fell without anyone firing a shot. Meanwhile, Benedict Arnold had led about 1,000 volunteers to Canada through Maine, across snowy country and along wild rivers. About a third of his force gave up and went home.

Together, Montgomery and Arnold attacked the fortress of Quebec on December 31, 1775. Montgomery was shot dead right at the start of the attack, which ended in a total defeat for the Americans.

Benedict Arnold died in Canada, after his act of treachery.

TIMELINE 1777 JULY–DECEMBER

KEY: Politics | Northern Campaign | Southern Campaign

July

July 6 New York
British occupy Fort Ticonderoga, having forced the Americans to abandon it.

August

August 4
General Horatio Gates replaces General Philip Schuyler as commander of the Northern Army.

August 6 New York
The Battle of Oriskany sees heavy casualties on both sides. The British move troops to leave the Patriots in control of the Mohawk Valley.

Canada Refuses to Join the War

The British, together with their Native American allies, had managed to keep control of Canada. George Washington sent a delegation to Montreal in 1776 to try to persuade the Canadians to join the Patriot cause, but it was unsuccessful. By the summer of that year, American armies had been forced to withdraw completely from Montreal and Canada after a British fleet sailed up the St. Lawrence River.

The Cost of Quebec

By keeping control of Canada, the British had preserved a base from which to attack New York and New England. After a failed campaign to control the Hudson River in 1777, they used the fortress at Quebec as a base for raiding operations into northern parts of the United States until the end of the war.

Quebec

British rule was not as unpopular in Quebec as the Americans thought. The British had allowed the French way of life to continue. Americans were outraged that a close neighbor could be French-speaking and Catholic. Perched on a rocky outcrop, Quebec was a strong fortress city. Although Arnold's force got inside the walls, further advances failed, and British troops were able to rally.

→ Quebec's position made it relatively easy to defend.

September 11 Pennsylvania
At the Battle of Brandywine, British defeat Washington and go on to occupy Philadelphia.

September 19 New York
In the first Battle of Saratoga, the Americans block the British advance.

October

October 4 Pennsylvania
The Americans fail to recapture Philadelphia from the British in the Battle of Germantown.

October 7 New York
At the second Battle of Saratoga, the British are forced to retreat. The American victory marks a turning point in the war.

December

December 18 Pennsylvania
The Continental army settles into its winter camp at Valley Forge.

The Green Mountain Boys

Originating in New Hampshire, this militia group played an important role in the Revolutionary War.

The Green Mountain Boys was the popular name for a militia formed in what is now the state of Vermont. In 1770, when the Green Mountain Boys came into existence, the area now called Vermont was known as the New Hampshire Grants. The Green Mountain Boys were led by Ethan Allen, and resisted attempts by the colony of New York to take control of the area they thought of as their own.

Taken Prisoner

Allen strongly supported the Patriots opposed to British rule. His Green Mountain Boys played a prominent role early in the American Revolution when they united with a Connecticut militia to capture Fort Ticonderoga, Crown Point, and Fort George from British forces in May 1775. Members of the Green Mountain Boys, including Allen himself, were captured when they failed to take Montreal in September 1775. Allen was eventually released in a prisoner exchange in 1778.

In 1777 Vermont had declared itself an independent republic, and the Green Mountain Boys became the standing army of the new institution. They played an important role in the defeat of British forces advancing from Canada under General Burgoyne at Saratoga in that same year.

KEY DATES

1765–1770 Ethan Allen becomes involved in disputes over an area known as the New Hampshire Grants. He forms the Green Mountain Boys as a local militia to intimidate those he considered his opponents.

May, 1775 Allen's Green Mountain Boys seize Fort Ticonderoga on Lake Champlain from the British. Allen loses his post as commander of the Boys to Seth Warner.

September, 1775 Allen takes part in a failed attack on Montreal. He is captured by the British.

1776 The Green Mountain Boys are effectively disbanded.

1777 Refounded as the Green Mountain Continental Rangers, the Green Mountain Boys take part in the battles of Hubbardton and Bennington. They are part of the forces of General Philip Schuyler.

1777 Vermont declares itself an independent state. Allen is paroled and is able to return to Vermont in 1778.

1 Ethan Allen is captured at Montreal. The failure to take Montreal was disappointing after earlier successes.

2 Fort Ticonderoga, the strategically valuable position on Lake Champlain that fell to the Green Mountain Boys.

3 A print of Ethan Allen surprising the garrison of Fort Ticonderoga and demanding their surrender.

4 The flag associated with the Green Mountain Boys. Today it is also the flag of the Vermont National Guard.

Civil War

As the thirteen colonies fought numerous battles against the British through 1776 and 1777, Congress issued a Declaration of Independence from British rule.

→ George Washington directs Patriot troops at the Battle of Princeton.

TIMELINE **1778 JANUARY–JUNE**

KEY: Politics | Northern Campaign | Southern Campaign

January

February 6 France
Treaty establishes commercial relations between France and United States.

March 13 England
French ambassador tells Britain that France now recognizes the United States as a country.

March 16 England
Peace commission set up in the House of Commons with American Patriots.

March 20 France
Benjamin Franklin presented to Louis XVI as France officially recognizes the United States.

British forces were often isolated defensive posts.

By early summer 1776, communities in Britain's North American colonies were divided. People who supported the rebellion against Parliament were known as "Patriots" or "Whigs." But many Americans refused to challenge the king's authority. They were called "Loyalists" or "Tories."

The British Plan

King George III and his ministers hoped that British forces could encourage Loyalists to fight against the Patriots. The British plan was to send a small army from Canada down Lake Champlain toward Albany, New York, gathering Loyalist support. Then a larger force would seize New York City. That would isolate New England from the rest of the colonies. Meanwhile, another small force would occupy Charleston, South Carolina, and link up with local Loyalist forces in the southern colonies. The plan soon went wrong. The attempt to

KEY DATES

June 28, 1776 The British fail to destroy Moultrie's Fort on Sullivan's Island off Charleston.

July 4, 1776 Declaration of Independence is approved.

August 27, 1776 The loss of New York City in the Battle of Long Island marks a low point for the Patriot cause.

October 11–13, 1776 The Battle of Valcour Island sets back Britain's attempt to split the colonies; it causes a delay that leads to military disaster at Saratoga.

December 26, 1776 After Washington crosses the Delaware River and defeats a Hessian force, Patriot morale receives a huge boost.

January 3, 1777 The Battle of Princeton. Washington turns the battle in the Patriots' favor and the British withdraw.

April

June

April 22–23 England John Paul Jones leads raids off the English coast.

May 20 Pennsylvania A British victory at the Battle of Barren Hill.

June 17 England A new war starts as France declares war on Great Britain.

June 19 Pennsylvania Washington's army leaves Valley Forge.

June 28 New Jersey The Battle of Monmouth Courthouse is the last major battle of the war in the northern states. It is a draw.

Lord Howe 1729–1814

Howe arrived in North America in 1775. He led the British forces that won a costly victory at Bunker Hill, and took over command of all British forces in September 1775. He enjoyed some success, taking back both New York and Philadelphia by 1777. However, his success in taking Philadelphia was counter balanced by his failure to assist General Burgoyne's advance south from Canada, which ended in defeat at Saratoga, a victory that persuaded France to enter the war. Howe resigned late in 1777.

William Howe had early successes in command of British forces in North America.

capture Charleston failed in June 1776. The army from Canada took too long to defeat American forces on Lake Champlain. Only the capture of New York City succeeded. The city's fall was a huge blow to the Patriots. Morale in parts of the Continental Army collapsed, and whole companies deserted. The New York area became a recruiting ground for Loyalists. Washington's remarkable recovery from the blow was early evidence that he was a leader with great qualities. A victory on December 26, 1776, at Trenton, New Jersey, revived Patriot hopes.

An American artillery unit comes under fire from the British at Fort Moultrie.

TIMELINE 1778 JULY–DECEMBER

KEY: Politics | Northern Campaign | Southern Campaign

July

July 2 Philadelphia
After British evacuate Philadelphia in June, Congress returns.

July 5 New York
Washington establishes his headquarters at West Point, a strategic point on the Hudson River.

August

July 29–August 31 Rhode Island
The Franco-American campaign ends in failure at the Battle of Rhode Island on August 29.

Washington Crossing the Delaware (Leutze, 1851) captured the fighting spirit of the Patriots.

Washington Crosses the Delaware

On Christmas Night 1776, George Washington and his men crossed the icy Delaware River. Correctly guessing the enemy would be celebrating, Washington and his men surprised enemy soldiers and scored an easy victory in the Battle of Trenton. This set up another victory against the British at Princeton, New Jersey. Trenton and Princeton ended a run of defeats that almost brought the American cause to an end and led the whole revolution to collapse.

The British Advance

In 1777, British troops from New York City were due to advance up the Hudson Valley to meet the British force from Canada at Albany. Instead, the forces in New York turned south to capture the Patriot capital at Philadelphia. American forces met the army from Canada at Saratoga and forced it to surrender. The defeat ended any hope the British had of being able to isolate New England from the rest of the colonies.

Declaring Independence

Meanwhile, the Continental Congress had issued the Declaration of Independence, setting out their grievances against the British government. The colonists had initially set out to defend their rights as Britons. Instead, they now saw that they had to become Americans, with their own nation. They began to seek support from other countries, particularly in Europe. The victory at Saratoga suggested that, with foreign support, their revolution might be successful.

November 11 New York
Loyalists and Indians kill more than 40 colonials during an encounter at Cherry Valley.

December

December 17 Illinois Country
The British recapture Fort Sackville in the Battle of Vincennes.

December 29 Georgia
British troops retake Savannah as the American troops are forced to retreat.

Spies and Spying

The Revolutionary War was not only fought on the battlefield. There was a secret war, too.

Spying and secret negotiations played an important part in the Revolutionary War. Both sides tried to find out the intentions and movements of their opponents. Because there was no certainty about what would happen after the war, many local people were prepared to talk to the British authorities. In 1778, George Washington set up a spy ring run by Captain Benjamin Tallmadge to find out information about the British in New York. This so-called Culper Ring discovered useful information. The most important was its uncovering of a plot organized by British spymaster Major John André for Benedict Arnold, who had been a successful Patriot commander. The plot was to surrender the fortress of West Point to the British. André was later hanged as a spy.

Negotiations in France

The British also had successful spies from Loyalist families. One such was Ann Bates, from Philadelphia. She used the fact that women were not considered dangerous to visit Washington's camp at White Plains in New York and deliver information on the state of his army to the British commander General Clinton.

Spying and secret communications also spread across the Atlantic. The Continental Congress kept its negotiations with France for assistance a secret, and its Committee of Secret Correspondence used an agent, Silas Deane, who claimed to be a merchant, as a go-between early in the war. Deane was one of the first spies to use invisible ink as a way of sending secret information back to the Continental Congress.

A British agent during the war later wrote: "Washington did not really outfight the British. He simply out-spied us."

KEY DATES

June, 1776 Washington asks John Jay to be head of New York's newly created Committee on Detecting and Defeating Conspiracies

September, 1776 Nathan Hale is hanged by the British for spying on their forces on Long Island. His last words were reported as, "I only regret that I have but one life to lose for my country."

1777 George Washington sends a letter to Colonel Elias Dayton, describing how, "The necessity of procuring good Intelligence is apparent and need not be further urged."

1777 Quaker Lydia Darragh overhears British officers planning a surprise attack on Patriot forces and crosses Philadelphia to warn them.

October 2, 1780 Major John André is hanged as a spy on Washington's orders.

1781 During the siege of Yorktown, James Armistead is a servant to British commander the Marquess of Cornwallis. He reports back to Lafayette on the state of the British army.

3

4

5

1 John Deane was supposedly a merchant but he was actually the bearer of messages back to the Continental Congress from France.

2 Major John André is stopped by Patriot militiamen near Tarrytown in New York. They find papers detailing a plot.

3 André is hanged on the orders of George Washington after the discovery of his communication with Benedict Arnold.

4 Benedict Arnold. He was in close contact with André in the plot to turn West Point (of which he was commander) over to the British.

5 John Jay was given what Washington considered to be the crucial post of heading a commission to root out spies in New York.

Battle of Saratoga

The American victory at Saratoga in October 1777 was the turning point in the war. The defeat of the British convinced foreign powers that the Americans might win.

General Burgoyne offers his sword in surrender to General Gates (center) at Saratoga.

TIMELINE 1779 JANUARY–JUNE

KEY: Politics | Northern Campaign | Southern Campaign

January

February 14 Georgia
American victory at the Battle of Kettle Creek is a Patriot morale booster.

March 3 Georgia
The British come back and win a victory at the Battle of Brier Creek.

May

May 10 New York
Benedict Arnold begins his discussions with British officers about going over to their side.

May–September New York
A Patriot expedition enters Indian territory to punish Native Americans for supporting the British.

In early 1777, the British commander General John Burgoyne devised a plan to isolate New England from the rest of the colonies. Two British armies would march south from Canada, while General Howe's army in the south would march northward. All three forces would meet at Albany, New York.

Trouble Ahead

Initially, Burgoyne's army of 8,000 troops advanced steadily into New York. Heavily outnumbered, the American commander, General Philip Schuyler, decided to abandon Fort Ticonderoga and concentrate on delaying tactics. The loss of the fort led the Continental Congress to replace Schuyler with General Horatio Gates. Still, Schuyler's tactics had slowed down Burgoyne's advance and allowed time for reinforcements to arrive.

By August, the British were suffering from supply problems. In western New York, the British advance from Fort Oswego was halted by General Benedict Arnold. Burgoyne's three-pronged attack on Albany had been greatly weakened. By September 1777, Patriot forces under Gates stood at 7,000 while British forces amounted to only 6,000.

KEY DATES

Early 1777 General Burgoyne plans to isolate New England from rest of the colonies.

August 1777 Supply problems hit advancing British troops.

September 13–14, 1777 Burgoyne crosses the Hudson River.

September 19, 1777 At the Battle of Freeman's Farm, an American victory is prevented by British and German discipline.

October 7, 1777 In further engagement, the British suffer losses three times as high as the Patriots; the British are forced to retreat three days later.

October 14, 1777 Burgoyne sends a letter of surrender.

October 17, 1777 Burgoyne finally surrenders at Saratoga.

← A revolutionary cannon still stands on the battlefield at Saratoga.

May 23 New York
Benedict Arnold gives the British valuable intelligence.

June

June 1 New York
The British are able to act on Arnold's intelligence, and Clinton begins offensive up the Hudson River.

June 20 South Carolina
Battle of Stono Ferry near Charleston sees an American attack repulsed.

John Burgoyne (1722–1792)

"Gentleman Johnny" was a leader of London society. He was a member of Parliament, playwright, and soldier. When he invaded New York in 1777, Burgoyne was confident of victory, but he made a fatal error. He moved his army too far from its supply bases and advanced too slowly. That allowed the Patriots to intercept him at the decisive Battle of Saratoga.

British Outnumbered

On September 13–14, Burgoyne crossed the Hudson River just north of Saratoga. On September 19, he engaged the Americans in battle at Freeman's Farm. Burgoyne's army was outnumbered by the Americans, but the superior discipline of the British and their German mercenaries (hired soldiers) was able to prevent an American victory. British losses numbered 600 casualties and prisoners, while the Americans suffered half that: 300 casualties.

Burgoyne's force retreated and fortified a position only a mile (1.6 km) from the Americans. Burgoyne learned that Sir Henry Clinton was leading 2,000 troops north to divert Gates' army. He decided to wait for Clinton's arrival, but American raids

➔ Burgoyne (in red coat) persuades Native Americans to support the British cause.

TIMELINE **1779 JULY–DECEMBER**

KEY: Politics | Northern Campaign | Southern Campaign

July

July 16 New York A U.S. victory at the Battle of Stony Point protects the key fortress of West Point.

August 14 Philadelphia Congress approves a peace proposal that calls for independence and for the British to leave North America.

September 23 North Sea American victory at the Battle of Flamborough Head is a blow to the reputation of Britain's Royal Navy.

September 27 Spain Spain refuses to recognize the United States as being a new republic.

reduced supplies and desertions increased. As the British force grew smaller, the arrival of American reinforcements swelled the Patriot forces to almost 11,000.

On October 7, Burgoyne sent 1,500 troops toward the American right flank. The Americans counterattacked at Bemis Heights. British losses of nearly 600 were three times those of the Patriots.

Defeat Beckons

With no aid from Clinton in sight, Burgoyne retreated north, reaching Saratoga on October 10. Gates's main force, now numbering 17,000, followed. Meanwhile, a 1,100-strong militia force crossed the Hudson River, cutting off any further retreat for the British. On October 14, Burgoyne wrote to Gates asking for terms of surrender. Hopeful that Clinton might still arrive, Burgoyne delayed before finally surrendering on October 17.

Horatio Gates (1727-1806)

Born in Essex, in England, Gates served in the British Army before becoming a planter in Virginia. He knew George Washington who recommended him for the Patriot army. He was in command of the Northern Department that defeated General Burgoyne at Saratoga in 1777. He was given command of the Southern Department in 1780 after the fall of Charles Town in May, but was much less successful, being defeated at the Battle of Camden in August.

← Horatio Gates was not offered another field command after his defeat at Camden in 1780.

October 9 Georgia
A Franco-American army attacks the British during the siege of Savannah; the British repulse the attack and manage to retain control of the city.

October — December

December 1 New Jersey
Washington establishes his winter quarters at Morristown; harsh conditions lead many of his troops to desert.

Valley Forge

Winter in the camp at Valley Forge saw Washington's Continental Army at a low point.

During the winter of 1777–1778, Washington's army moved into quarters in Valley Forge. Although it had defeated the British at the Battle of Saratoga in October, it had lost Philadelphia and was unable to take it back. Washington's army was in poor condition. His soldiers built some 1,500 huts and cabins to live in, but the army consisted of 12,000 men and the supplies necessary to provision them did not get through. Some supplies had been stored at Valley Forge over the summer but these had been destroyed by a British raid in September. The men were short of food and clothing. The French general Lafayette described how "the unfortunate soldiers were in want of everything; they had neither coats, hats, shirts, nor shoes; their feet and legs froze till they had become almost black."

Discipline and Drill

Diseases such as typhus ravaged the soldiers and up to 2,000 may have died. However, the time spent in these difficult conditions was not wasted. A Prussian officer, Baron Friedrich von Steuben, drilled the soldiers in European maneuvers and fighting with bayonets. This training was seen to bear fruit at the Battle of Monmouth in June 1778, when the Continental Army fought for over five hours against British troops and proved that they were able to stand and fight in a pitched battle against European professional troops.

KEY DATES

September 18, 1777 German troops fighting with the British forces destroy supplies stored at Valley Forge. The British take Philadelphia.

December 19, 1777 Washington's army reaches Valley Forge, where it prepares winter quarters. The area is chosen partly because it is close to Philadelphia and can inhibit British raids into the Pennsylvania countryside.

December 23, 1777 Washington writes how he has had to quell a "dangerous mutiny" because of the lack of adequate food for his troops.

January 24, 1778 A delegation from the Continental Congress witnesses the supply problems at Valley Forge.

March, 1778 Washington persuades Nathanael Greene to become Quartermaster General of the Continental Army to deal with supply problems.

May 6, 1778 The troops at Valley Forge learn of the alliance with France. In celebration they fire volleys with their muskets and receive extra rum rations.

1 Baron Friedrich von Steuben. Some soldiers of the Continental Army resented his drill practice, but it stood them in good stead.

2 Washington and Lafayette inspecting the troops at Valley Forge during the bitter winter of 1777–1778.

3 A replica of one of the cabins that Washington's army built at Valley Forge to give them some protection against the cold.

4 A print of the Battle of Monmouth, where the Continental Army showed that Baron Steuben's drill had not been wasted.

5 Nathanael Greene. Although Greene was reluctant, Washington eventually persuaded him to take the post of Quartermaster General.

International War

In 1778, the Revolutionary War became an international conflict as France and Spain, both old enemies of Britain, joined the American cause.

HMS *Quebec* explodes during a battle with the French frigate *Surveillante* off France in October 1779.

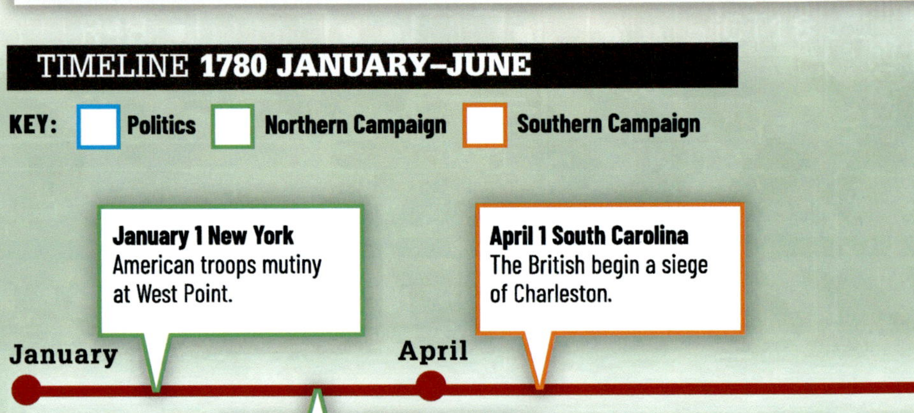

TIMELINE 1780 JANUARY–JUNE

KEY: Politics | Northern Campaign | Southern Campaign

January

January 1 New York
American troops mutiny at West Point.

January 16 Spanish Waters
First Battle of Trafalgar sees British defeat an inferior Spanish squadron.

April

April 1 South Carolina
The British begin a siege of Charleston.

France and Spain had old rivalries with Great Britain. Both hoped that the war in North America would bring a chance to win back territory they had lost to the British in wars earlier in the 1700s.

France and Spain Join the Cause

America's alliance with France was the result of months of diplomacy. Benjamin Franklin had arrived in Paris, the French capital, at the end of 1776 on a mission from Congress. Franklin offered the French an opportunity to avenge its losses to the British in Canada and elsewhere in 1763, at the end of the French and Indian War. The French government gave the Americans a huge amount of cash to buy weapons and loaned them money that was vital for the American cause during the winter of 1776–1777.

Spain was slower to join the war. The Spanish government was worried that the example of the

← *Spirit of 76* (Patriot musicians painted by Archibald Willard in 1875) was originally titled *Yankee Doodle*.

KEY DATES

June 28, 1778 The Battle of Monmouth Courthouse, the last major clash in the northern states, ends as a draw.

July 16, 1779 American victory at the Battle of Stony Point.

September 23, 1779 HMS *Serapis* surrenders at the Battle of Flamborough Head.

September-October 1779 Siege of Savannah ends in British victory.

May 12, 1780 Charleston falls to the British.

August 16, 1780 General Horatio Gates flees during the Battle of Camden.

October 7, 1780 Loyalists surrender at the Battle of King's Mountain.

May 12 South Carolina The worst American defeat of the Revolution as Charleston surrenders. British capture over 3,000 Patriots.

June

May 29 South Carolina Loyalists meet Patriots at Waxhaws in Lancaster. Patriots claim Loyalists attacked them as they tried to surrender.

Molly Pitcher

The wives of soldiers often traveled with their husbands. Some helped on the battlefield. At Monmouth, Mary Hays McCauly earned the nickname "Molly Pitcher" by bringing pitchers of water to the thirsty soldiers. She helped carry the wounded to safety. When her husband was injured, Molly took his place. She helped to load and fire a cannon for the rest of the battle. Molly's bravery was recognized by George Washington, who made her a noncommissioned officer.

"Sergeant" Molly Pitcher at the Battle of Monmouth.

Washington rallies his troops at the Battle of Monmouth.

Patriots might encourage discontent in its own colonies. The Spanish did not want to encourage revolution in Mexico, Colombia, or Peru, because Spain relied on money from the colonies. However, in 1779, the Spanish began to attack British forces. They concentrated on Florida, which then reached west to the Mississippi River.

A Different Strategy

Foreign support encouraged American leaders to revise their plans. American military strategy would now focus on limiting British control to the areas immediately around the ports of New York and Newport, Rhode Island, from where they had little prospect of breaking

TIMELINE 1780 JULY–DECEMBER

KEY: Politics | Northern Campaign | Southern Campaign

July — October

July 25 North Carolina
General Horatio Gates takes command of Southern Army at Coxe's Hill.

July 30 South Carolina
The capture of Thicketty Fort (Fort Anderson) precedes the Battle of King's Mountain.

August 16 South Carolina
At the Battle of Camden, General Gates flees, ruining his reputation. British confirm their control of South Carolina.

out. At the same time, Patriot commanders sought to exert control north of the Ohio River during the Illinois Campaign.

British Change Tactics

The British decided that it was impossible to defeat the Americans in New England and the Middle Atlantic states. They withdrew their troops from Philadelphia. British leaders looked to the South. Lord George Germain, secretary of state for America, believed that Loyalists in the Carolinas and Georgia would rally to the king if a British army landed there. In 1778, the British attacked Savannah, Georgia, starting a new phase of the war. Victories at Savannah and at the siege of Charleston would see the British eventually extend control over much of the South.

The Fall of Charleston

The British strategy of attacking the southern colonies bore fruit in 1780 when Lord Cornwallis took Charles Town (now Charleston). His troops laid siege to the town from March 1780 to May, and the Patriot commander Benjamin Lincoln was forced to surrender over 5,000 men. Cornwallis promised the slaves of rebels that they would be given their freedom, and this brought in many new recruits. He also recruited "Tories," Americans loyal to George III.

British troops start the bombardment of the fortifications of Charles Town.

October 7 South Carolina
Battle of King's Mountain sees British invasion of North Carolina abandoned as Loyalist troops surrender.

December

December 21 England
Britain declares war on the Netherlands after the Dutch join the League of Armed Neutrality.

John Paul Jones

Although he was a prickly character, John Paul Jones was an excellent naval commander.

Often called the "Father of the American Navy," naval officer John Paul Jones (1747–1792) had left his native Scotland after killing one of his seamen with a sword. As this incident may suggest, he had a short temper and often fell out with other members of his crew and his superiors. He arrived in the colony of Virginia in 1775. Experienced naval officers were in demand, and he was given command of the USS *Alfred*, a 24-gun frigate, in December 1775. He then helped in a raid on Nassau in the Bahamas. Over the next year he captured several vessels on behalf of the Continental Congress, and he later sailed to France, where his ship the USS *Ranger* was saluted by the French Navy after the signing of the alliance between the two countries.

1

Victory over *Serapis*

Jones raided British ports on the Irish Sea and then captured the sloop *Drake*. In 1779, commanding the 42-gun USS *Bonhomme Richard*, he led a squadron into the North Sea to engage Royal Navy vessels in the Battle of Flamborough Head. Despite being heavily outgunned, Jones refused to surrender his vessel and he captured the British 50-gun frigate *Serapis* as well as another Royal Navy vessel. For this victory, Jones was designated a "Chevalier" (Knight) by the King of France.

Jones later served for a few years in the Russian Navy, but after disagreements with some members of the aristocracy he returned to France in 1790 and died in Paris in 1792.

2

3

KEY DATES

July 6, 1747 John Paul Jones is born in Kirkcudbrightshire, Scotland. His baptismal name was simply John Paul. He added Jones at a later date.

December 7, 1775 Jones is appointed a lieutenant in the newly formed Continental Navy.

November 1, 1777 Jones sails for France. He commands raids on Scotland and Ireland in 1778.

September 23, 1779 Having taken command of the *Bonhomme Richard*, Jones takes part in the battle of Flamborough Head. His ship is badly damaged but when asked to strike his colors (a signal of surrender) he replies, "I may sink, but I'll be damned if I strike."

1787 Jones joins the Russian Imperial Navy, where he reaches the rank of rear admiral.

July 18, 1792 John Paul Jones dies in Paris.

4

5

1 John Paul Jones was a forceful commander and was never prepared to withdraw from a fight.

2 A contemporary painting of the battle between *Bonhomme Richard* and the Royal Navy frigate *Serapis*.

3 A British cartoon portraying Jones as a pirate because of his swashbuckling activities attacking British ports and merchant vessels.

4 The port of Whitehaven in the north of England was attacked by Jones in 1778, but the attack was unsuccessful.

5 The statue in Washington, D.C., which commemorates Jones' key role in the creation of the U.S. Navy.

End of the War

As the British found themselves fighting the French and Spanish as well as the Americans, their resources became stretched and the war moved in America's favor.

A cabin stands on the preserved site of the Cowpens battlefield.

TIMELINE 1781 JANUARY–JUNE

KEY: Politics | Northern Campaign | Southern Campaign

January

January 1-10 New Jersey
Patriot mutiny sees almost half the troops leave the army.

January 17 South Carolina
American victory at the Battle of Cowpens boosts morale. British attempts to control western South Carolina have now come to an end.

March 9-May 8 Florida
Battle of Pensacola ends with the Spanish retaking Florida from the British.

March 15 North Carolina
British victory at the Battle of Guilford Courthouse becomes a strategic defeat as Cornwallis is forced to retreat to the coast at Wilmington.

By 1779, the American army had developed a full range of uniforms.

With France already fighting on the American side, Spain and the Netherlands both joined the war on the American side in 1779. Both hoped that victory would bring the chance to gain foreign colonies.

The British Make Gains

In America, the British remained besieged in New York, but they fared better elsewhere. They took Charleston and narrowly failed to capture a key fort at West Point on the Hudson River. But then the one-time American hero General Benedict Arnold switched sides and tried to hand the fort to the British. In the South, Patriot militias had more success than the regulars commanded by Horatio Gates, who was replaced by Nathanael Greene at the command of Washington in fall 1780.

KEY DATES

January 17, 1781 Victory at the Battle of the Cowpens boosts Patriot morale.

March 15, 1781 The British General Lord Cornwallis is forced to retreat to the coast at Wilmington after the Battle of Guilford Courthouse.

April 25, 1781 The troops of the Prussian American General von Steuben are outnumbered and forced to retreat during the Battle of Petersburg.

March 9–May 8, 1781 At the Battle of Pensacola, Spain takes back Florida, which the British have held since the end of the French and Indian War in 1763.

September 8, 1781 At the Battle of Eutaw Springs, the Americans suffer heavy casualties before they retreat; the British, under Colonel Stewart, withdraw into Charleston, leaving South Carolina in Patriot hands.

April

June

April 25 Virginia
At the Battle of Petersburg, outnumbered American militias are forced to retreat across the Appomattox River.

May 22–June 19 South Carolina
The siege of Ninety-Six is an unsuccessful Patriot attack on a Loyalist stronghold.

Loyalists in the South

The British had counted on there being strong support for the king and for continuing British rule in the southern colonies, but they found fewer recruits than they had hoped. There was also mutual mistrust between the Loyalists (called "Tories" by Patriots) and British army officers. After the war, many Loyalists in the southern colonies went to Florida.

Patriot Mutiny

On January 1, 1781, harsh winter conditions sparked the only major Patriot mutiny of the war. Around 1,500 soldiers from Pennsylvania insisted that their service was over. They marched to Philadelphia and asked Congress to discharge them. Two hundred were discharged while the remainder were given a furlough—or rest—and then sent back to the army.

Fortunes Begin to Change

The British troops found themselves increasingly stretched as they had to fight the French and Spanish for control of islands in the Caribbean as well as on the American continent. They lost

➔ Britannia offers money and help to exiled Loyalists in this 1783 engraving.

TIMELINE 1781 JULY–DECEMBER

KEY: Politics | Northern Campaign | Southern Campaign

July

August 1 Virginia
General Cornwallis establishes British base at Yorktown on Chesapeake Bay.

September 5–8 Virginia
British naval vessels are forced to retreat in the Battle of Virginia Capes fought in waters off Yorktown.

September 8 South Carolina
British withdraw after the Battle of Eutaw Springs, leaving South Carolina in Patriot hands.

September 28 Virginia
Siege of Yorktown begins as Washington's army surrounds Cornwallis's new base.

Patriots force back British redcoats at the Battle of the Cowpens.

West Florida to the Spanish in the Battle of Pensacola, when the besieging Spanish blasted a hole in the walls of a British fort.

Victories on the mainland were proving costly in terms of casualties, meanwhile, so British forces planned to withdraw to coastal positions to await reinforcements. Those reinforcements were prevented by a French blockade off the Atlantic coast. The blockade also stopped supplies from England from reaching the troops. Numerous battles fought across the Carolinas in the South eventually drove the British into a trap at Yorktown—and a defeat that would mark the end of the Revolutionary War.

Spain in the Revolutionary War

In 1779, Spain joined the American cause, despite worries that its colonies might want independence. Spain wanted to take back Florida, which it lost to Britain after defeat in the Seven Years' War. The Spanish gave money and supplies to the Patriots and let them use the port of New Orleans. Spanish military and naval forces were active against the British and their allies in Florida and the Southeast.

Benjamin Franklin gained essential French support for the American cause.

October

December

October 3 Virginia
Skirmish at Gloucester is part of the Yorktown campaign as British and French troops clash.

October 17 Virginia
Realizing his troops are beaten, Cornwallis proposes the terms of his surrender.

October 19 Virginia
Cornwallis's surrender virtually ensures success for American independence.

Marquis de Lafayette

Lafayette was a French nobleman who played an important part in both the American and French Revolutions.

Gilbert du Motier, Marquis de Lafayette (1757–1834) was a French nobleman. He came from a military family and had been commissioned as an officer when he was just 13 years old. He became a member of the Freemasons, a secret society that was in favor of reforms. He expressed support for the Patriot cause as early as September 1775, partly because of his liberal sympathies and partly because of his anti-British feeling.

Arrival in America

Lafayette met the American secret agent Silas Deane and asked to be sent to North America. He arrived there in June 1777 onboard a ship with a cargo of arms that he had personally funded. He met George Washington in August that year, and the two men got along well. As a result, Lafayette was given senior commands in the Continental Army. He was wounded at the Battle of Brandywine in September but managed to lead his men from the field in good order.

After a period back in France, Lafayette returned to North America in 1780 with the promise of French troops and a fleet to help the Patriot cause. He played an important part in the campaign that led to the British surrender at Yorktown. After the war, Lafayette campaigned for an end to slavery. He went on to play an important part in the French Revolution of 1789 and was active in French politics until the 1830s.

KEY DATES

September 6, 1757 Lafayette is born in Chavaniac, France.

August 5, 1777 Lafayette meets George Washington for the first time. The two men become friends. Like Lafayette, Washington is a Freemason.

October, 1778 Lafayette returns home to France on leave. He is awarded a Sword of Honor by the Continental Congress.

April 27, 1780 Lafayette returns to North America, having secured a promise from the French king that 6,000 French soldiers would be sent to aid the Patriot cause.

August, 1781 Lafayette's forces in Virginia pin down a British army under Cornwallis. Washington arrives with major reinforcements and a French fleet drives off the Royal Navy. Trapped, Cornwallis is forced to surrender in the decisive battle of the Revolutionary War.

May 20, 1834 Lafayette dies in Paris, France.

1 Lafayette is wounded at the Battle of Brandywine. Despite his wound he stayed on the field and rallied his men.

2 The young French nobleman wearing the uniform of an officer in the Continental Army, where he served with distinction.

3 A 19th-century painting of George Washington and Lafayette at Mount Vernon in 1784, after independence had been secured.

4 Lafayette in 1791, in the uniform of a lieutenant colonel of the French army.

Battle of Yorktown

The Battle of Yorktown was the last major battle of the Revolutionary War. With the surrender of General Lord Cornwallis, the British knew they had lost their colonies.

This engraving shows the British trapped by the Continental Army on land and French ships off the coast.

TIMELINE **1782 JANUARY–JUNE**

KEY: Politics | Northern Campaign | Southern Campaign

January

February 17–June 20 Indian Ocean
The French and British clash at sea in four separate engagements.

March

March 22 Kentucky
Americans fight Indians in the Battle of Little Mountain.

Although the British won almost all the battles in the Carolinas, they suffered considerable losses of men, supplies, and equipment. Their hopes of recruiting local Loyalists to swell the army's numbers failed to materialize. Few joined up, and even fewer stayed for long.

After another costly victory at Guilford Courthouse on March 15, 1781, Cornwallis marched to Wilmington on the coast of North Carolina to pick up supplies and reinforcements. Next month, he took about 1,500 men north to Petersburg, Virginia, where, on May 20, they linked up with 6,000 others led by the former Patriot hero Benedict Arnold. The British then moved to the area around Portsmouth and Williamsburg in Virginia.

A Plan for Attack

Cornwallis had orders to set up a naval base for an attack on Virginia. He selected a site at Yorktown, at the south end of Chesapeake Bay.

KEY DATES

August 30, 1781 A French fleet arrives off Yorktown to blockade Chesapeake Bay.

September 5, 1781 In the Battle of Virginia Capes, the French fleet defeats the British under Admiral Thomas Graves.

September 28–October 19, 1781 Three weeks of heavy bombardment and the capture of key forward positions sees the British forced to surrender.

October 19, 1781 Cornwallis surrenders to Washington.

October 24, 1781 Clinton's fleet arrives off Yorktown too late to help Cornwallis.

French ships blockaded the British position at Yorktown.

May

June

May 25–June 6 Ohio Country
Washington asks Colonel William Crawford to lead an expedition into Ohio.

June 6 Ohio Country
Crawford's supply train is attacked; in the ensuing battle 250 Patriots die.

June 20 Philadelphia
The Continental Congress adopts the Great Seal of the United States.

Comte de Rochambeau

Jean-Baptiste Donatien de Vimeur, Count of Rochambeau, commanded the military force sent from France to cooperate with the Continental Army in 1780. He had served with the French army in Europe, but had been wounded in battle. Rochambeau played a key role in the defeat of the British at Yorktown. Although he was a more experienced soldier, Rochambeau was careful to acknowledge that Washington was overall commander of the allied forces.

At Yorktown, the British began building defensive works. Cornwallis knew that while he waited for reinforcements to arrive by sea he would have to withstand a siege from troops commanded by Washington's lieutenant, the Marquis de Lafayette.

The French Help Out

The first fleet to arrive in the area was French. Some 24 ships and 3,000 troops established a blockade across the mouth of Chesapeake Bay. This was a decisive blow: it ensured that Cornwallis's wait for reinforcements would be in vain. That gave George Washington the freedom to march 7,000 American and French troops

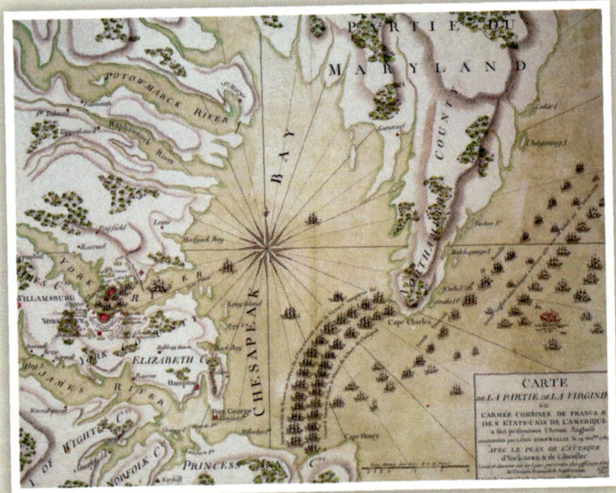

➔ This French map shows the position of the opposing sides at Yorktown.

TIMELINE **1782 JULY–DECEMBER**

KEY: Politics | Northern Campaign | Southern Campaign

July

July 11 Georgia
British governor Sir James Wright and other British officials evacuate Savannah.

September

September 3 Paris
Preliminary peace negotiations, ongoing since 1780, end. Key details, including independence, still have to be resolved.

September 11–13 West Virginia
Loyalists besiege group of Americans at the Siege of Fort Henry (Wheeling).

south from New York, giving the Patriots a considerable advantage in numbers.

The British Are Surrounded

With Washington and Lafayette blocking the way south and Rochambeau's French straddling the road west to Williamsburg, Cornwallis had no way out. He was outnumbered, and food supplies were running low. He tried to get men across the York River to Gloucester. Some made it, but a storm scattered their boats. Meanwhile, the arrival of British reinforcements had been delayed. On October 24 a fleet of 16 ships and 7,000 soldiers under General Henry Clinton finally arrived off Yorktown. But by then it was too late. Cornwallis had surrendered his whole army to George Washington on October 19.

Peace Negotiations

In March 1782, a new government took office in London. Within a month, the first contact was made between the American diplomat Benjamin Franklin and his British counterpart, Richard Oswald. The two men met in Paris. In September, full negotiations began and a treaty was agreed to in November of that year. The Americans would not approve a final treaty until the British had also come to an agreement with their French allies over territorial disputes and other claims.

← Cornwallis rides through the American lines to surrender.

October

October 20 Morocco
The Spanish attempt to retake the southern fortress of Gibraltar from the British—their reason for entering the war—in the naval Battle of Cape Spartel.

November 4 South Carolina
The encounter at John's Ferry, a successful assault on a British foraging party, is one of the war's last actions.

December

December 14 South Carolina
The evacuation of Charleston leaves no British troops in the South.

Aftermath of the War

After the fighting finished, it took many years before America established itself as an independent nation free from the shackles of British colonial rule.

George Washington addresses the Constitutional Convention in 1787.

TIMELINE 1783 JANUARY–JUNE

KEY: Politics | Northern Campaign | Southern Campaign

January

February 4 London
King George III issues proclamation of cessation of hostilities, ending the Revolutionary War.

February 6 Spain
Spain ends the siege of Gibraltar.

March 15 New York
Washington confronts a group of mutinous officers in his Newburgh Address.

April 15 Philadelphia
Congress ratifies preliminary peace treaty signed in November 1782.

After the U.S. Constitution had been drafted, George Washington became the first president of the United States in 1789. He served until 1797, trying to enhance unity among Americans while also creating national institutions, such as a national bank.

The United States faced many problems at the end of the war. The British still controlled important trading posts in the Great Lakes area, such as Detroit. The war had cost over $3 million, which still had to be paid. Yet there was no easy way for Congress to raise money. It could ask the states for contributions, but it had no way of forcing them to pay.

New Laws

One key success for Congress came in the Northwest Territory, which covered the area around the Great Lakes north of the Ohio River. Congress passed a law known as the Northwest Ordinance Act of 1787. This act arranged for the sale of land in the region,

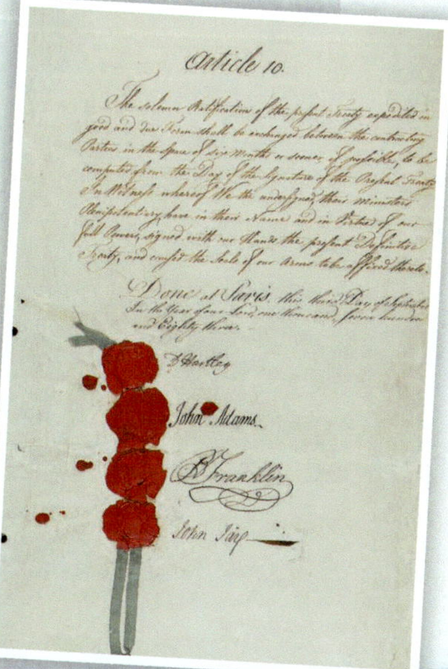

Article 10.

The solemn Ratification of the present Treaty expedited in good and due Form shall be exchanged between the contracting Parties in the Space of Six Months or sooner if possible, to be computed from the Day of the Signature of the present Treaty. In Witness whereof We the undersigned their Ministers Plenipotentiary have in their Name and in Virtue of our full Powers, signed with our Hands the present Definitive Treaty, and caused the Seals of our Arms to be affixed thereto.

Done at Paris, this third Day of September, In the Year of our Lord one thousand seven hundred and Eighty three.

D Hartley

John Adams.

B Franklin

John Jay

The Treaty of Paris ended the Revolutionary War.

KEY DATES

August 1786–February 1787 Shays' Rebellion leads to changes in the new written Constitution.

May 17, 1787 Delegates at Constitutional Convention in Philadelphia agree new Constitution.

July 13, 1787 The Northwest Ordinance Act allows for westward U.S. expansion.

April 30, 1789 Washington inaugurated as the first president.

June 18, 1812–February 18, 1815 America and Britain fight the War of 1812.

August 24, 1814 British troops set fire to the new American capital, Washington, D.C.

December 24, 1814 America and Britain sign a peace treaty. in Ghent, Belgium.

April

April 17 Arkansas Spanish soldiers defeat British partisans at Fort Carlos.

April 19 New York Washington informs the troops of the Continental army that hostilities have ended.

June

June 8 New York Washington sends a circular letter preparing to disband his army.

June 16 Philadelphia Mutinous soldiers march on the capital demanding back pay; Congress flees to Princeton, New Jersey.

its government as a territory of the United States, its eventual statehood, and the abolition of slavery within its boundaries. After a war against Native Americans living in the area and negotiations with Britain, American control and settlement were confirmed by 1797.

The financial crisis was less easily solved. Congress could not pay the interest on its debts or pay the money owed to the people who had fought in the war. In 1786, a former army captain, Daniel Shays, led a rebellion in western Massachusetts.

Loyalists in Canada

Many Loyalists lost their property when state governments took it to reward Patriots. Some 70,000 of the 100,000 Loyalists who left the United States settled in Canada, where the British set up the province of New Brunswick for them. Others, including Native American allies, settled in what is now Ontario. A third area for settlement was southern Quebec, near the American border.

→ Washington celebrates his inauguration as the first president in 1789.

New Constitution

Shays' Rebellion, along with fears over the debt, led to the calling of a convention in Philadelphia to amend the Articles of Confederation. Instead, the convention wrote a new Constitution, which was agreed to by enough of the thirteen states in 1788 to create a new government. The bloodshed of Shays' Rebellion led the delegates to think

TIMELINE 1783 JULY-DECEMBER

KEY: Politics | Northern Campaign | Southern Campaign

July

September 3 Paris
The peace treaty is signed, formally ending the war and recognizing United States as an independent nation.

October

October 20 Philadelphia
Congress votes to build a "federal" capital on the banks of the Potomac River.

October 23 Virginia
Virginia frees slaves who fought in the war.

Lafayette became an American hero for his role at Yorktown.

carefully about how to stop the new country from falling into anarchy during times of crisis. Congress now had the right to raise taxes, the same power that had caused the British colonies to rebel in the first place.

Rebellions Continue

Washington appointed the war veteran Alexander Hamilton as the first secretary of the treasury. He encouraged Congress to use its powers to raise money to pay the national debt. He created the first national bank and charged tariffs on imports. Hamilton also placed a tax on whiskey. It was highly unpopular. In 1794, protestors rebelled against the tax in Pennsylvania. Washington led a large militia force to put down the revolt. The United States had not seen its last struggle over taxes.

The War of 1812

The Revolutionary War was not the last time Britain and the United States went to war. In 1812, they fought over the right of the British to search for smugglers on American ships on the high seas. In 1814, British troops set fire to the new capital, Washington, D.C. Both sides found the war expensive and with no gain to either. A peace treaty was signed at Ghent, in Belgium, in December 1814.

Citizens fight fires after a British attack on the White House in 1812.

November 3 New York
The Continental Army is disbanded at Newburgh.

November 25 New York
The British army evacuates New York City, its last military base in the United States.

December

December 4 New York
Washington bids farewell to his officers in the Fraunces Tavern in New York City.

December 23 Virginia
Washington resigns as commander in chief and returns to his estate, Mount Vernon.

Glossary

artillery Cannons and other heavy gunpowder weapons.

assembly The elected representative body of one of the British colonies in North America.

blockade A barrier of naval ships that prevents other vessels sailing to or from a coast or a particular port.

colonist Someone who lives in a colony, a territory ruled by another country.

congress A formal assembly where representatives from different bodies discuss problems.

desert To abandon one's military service without permission.

dissent Disagreement with someone else's views.

flank The exposed side of a military force.

governor An official who governed an American colony on behalf of the British king.

Loyalists The name given to Americans who supported British government of North America; also known as "Tories."

mercenary A professional soldier who will fight for whoever pays him or her to do so.

militia A body of armed civilians who are trained to fight in times of emergency.

Minutemen Elite members of the colonial militia, who were named for their ability to be ready to fight at a moment's notice.

morale The positive spirit that enables soldiers and civilians to do difficult tasks, such as fighting.

Patriots American supporters of the fight for independence; also known as "Whigs."

peninsula A narrow piece of land that juts into a body of water.

redcoat A soldier in the British army, named for the color of his uniform jacket.

siege A battle in which an enemy force surrounds a city or other position and waits until it is forced to surrender.

silversmith A craftsman who makes jewelry and other objects from silver.

traitor Someone who commits treason by betraying his or her own country.

Further Resources

Books

American Battlefield Trust. *Battle Maps of the American Revolution.* Knox Press, 2022.

Barbieri, Brooke. *Boston in the American Revolution.* The History Press, 2017.

Finch, Fletcher C. *The American Revolutionary War (Considering Different Options).* Rosen Publishing, 2019.

History For Kids. *Road to Independence.* Dinobibi Publishing, 2019.

Hourly History. *Boston Tea Party.* Hourly History, 2021.

McClafferty, Carla Killough. *Spies in the American Revolution for Kids.* Rockridge Press, 2021.

Smith, Elliott. *Hidden Heroes of the Revolutionary War.* Lerner Publishing Group, 2023.

Smithsonian Institution. *Eyewitness: The American Revolution.* Dorling Kindersley, 2022.

Trusiani, Lisa. *The Story of George Washington.* Rockridge Press, 2020.

Various. *America's Founding Documents.* Lerner Publishing Group, 2018.

Websites

www.pbs.org/ktca/liberty/
The companion site for the PBS series *Liberty! The American Revolution.*

www.kidinfo.com/american_history/american_revolution.html
Kidinfo list of links to Revolutionary War sites.

www.battlefields.org/learn/revolutionary-war
American Battlefield Trust guide to the key engagements of the war.

www.historyplace.com/unitedstates/revolution/index.html
The History Place timelines of the Revolutionary War.

https://www.ducksters.com/history/american_revolution.php
Learn more about the American Revolution with the Ducksters team!

Index